JENSEN HUANG

Visionary of Silicon Valley - The Life and Times of a Tech Innovator

Felicia Cort

Copyright @ 2024 By Felicia Cort

All rights reserved. No part of this book may be reproduced, distributed, or transmitted in any form or by any means, including photocopying, recording, or other electronic or mechanical methods, without the prior written permission of the publisher, except in the case of brief quotations embodied in critical reviews and specific other noncommercial uses permitted by copyright law.

This book is a work of fiction. Names, characters, places, and incidents either are products of the author's imagination or are used fictitiously. Any resemblance to actual events or locales or persons, living or dead, is entirely coincidental.

Disclaimer

The following book is for entertainment and informational purposes only. The information presented is without contract or any type of guarantee assurance. While every caution has been taken to provide accurate and current information, it is solely the reader's responsibility to check all information contained in this article before relying upon it. Neither the author nor the publisher can be held accountable for any errors or omissions. Under no circumstances will any legal responsibility or blame be held against the author or publisher for any reparation, damages, or monetary loss due to the information presented, either directly or indirectly. This book is not intended as legal or medical advice. If any such specialized advice is needed, seek a qualified individual for help.

Trademarks are used without permission. Use of the trademark is not authorized by, associated with, or sponsored by the trademark owners. All trademarks and brands used within this book are used with no intent to infringe on the trademark owners and are only used for clarifying purposes. This book is not sponsored by or affiliated with tech innovation, its companies, the innovators, or anyone involved with them.

Table of Content

INTRODUCTION
7

CHAPTER 1: EARLY LIFE AND ACADEMIC PURSUITS   13

CHAPTER 2: THE STANFORD CHAPTER
26

CHAPTER 3: EARLY CAREER AND INDUSTRY INSIGHTS   33

CHAPTER 4: THE BIRTH OF INNOVATION
40

CHAPTER 5: THE RISE OF THE GPU
48

CHAPTER 6: LEADERSHIP AND INNOVATION
55

CHAPTER 7: EXPANDING HORIZONS
61

CHAPTER 8: CHALLENGES AND CONTROVERSIES
67

CHAPTER 9: RECOGNITION AND LEGACY
73
CONCLUSION
78

INTRODUCTION

Stories of bold visionaries who dared to dream large and use technology to alter the world abound in Silicon Valley annals. Jensen Huang, the co-founder and CEO of NVIDIA—a name linked to innovation in computer graphics and artificial intelligence—is one of these notables. Huang has brought NVIDIA to the forefront of the industry and completely changed the face of modern computing with his unrelenting faith in the potential of technology, strategic leadership, and contagious excitement.

This book explores Jensen Huang's amazing journey from an inquisitive young mind captivated by electronics to a visionary leader at the head of a tech titan. It is an engrossing read. We'll look at his crucial influence on how GPUs (Graphics Processing Units), which were formerly thought of as niche parts for gamers, evolved into potent workhorses that fueled breakthroughs in science, medicine, and even the creation of self-driving automobiles.

Still, there is much more to the Jensen Huang and NVIDIA tale than just graphics. Huang's great insight allowed him to see GPUs' enormous potential as the best platform for training intricate AI models. This tactical change catapulted NVIDIA to the vanguard of the artificial intelligence revolution, as their GPUs enabled the creation of ground-breaking applications in domains as disparate as robotics, computer vision, and natural language processing.

There is no denying the influence of NVIDIA's innovations. The company's technology is changing how we live, work, and interact with the world around us. It is speeding up drug development and tailored medicine and enabling the creation of immersive virtual experiences. This book will examine these varied uses, demonstrating the significant impact of NVIDIA's work on a range of spheres in our lives.

But there are difficulties along the way. Careful thought must be given to ethical issues about privacy, addiction, and potential socioeconomic injustices as NVIDIA explores unexplored areas like the metaverse. The book will explore these intricacies, looking at how NVIDIA is attempting to ensure that its technology is developed responsibly and tackling these issues.

In the end, this book is more than just a history of NVIDIA's accomplishments or a biography of Jensen Huang. It's a tale about the responsibility that comes with using technology, the transformational force of invention, and the value of visionary leadership. We may learn important lessons from Huang's path and the influence of NVIDIA that will motivate and encourage the next generation of leaders, innovators, and entrepreneurs to dream big, question the status quo, and work toward building a better future for everybody.

The engrossing tale that takes place inside these pages is set up by this introduction. We will learn more about the guy who started the revolution, the business he founded, and their enormous influence on the technology industry as we delve deeper into Jensen Huang's life and work.

The story that takes shape in these pages goes beyond a simple biography or academic manual. This engrossing investigation delves into human resourcefulness, the unwavering quest for a goal, and the significant influence technology may yield when directed by accountability and a yearning for constructive transformation.

The first few chapters explore the early years of Jensen Huang, detailing his passion for electronics at a young age and his unwavering commitment to education. We see how his early curiosity developed into a thorough comprehension of computer science and engineering, setting the stage for his subsequent successes. Next, we delve into the history of NVIDIA, a firm that was founded by Huang and his fellow founders to revolutionize computer graphics and realize the full potential of GPUs.

The book explores the technological innovations that NVIDIA under Huang's direction has been leading. We look at how GPUs have developed from specialized gaming hardware to flexible computing systems that can handle intricate scientific simulations, speed up financial modeling, and even enable the production of incredibly lifelike virtual environments. This investigation delves beyond technical details to emphasize the practical uses of NVIDIA's technology and the revolution it has brought about across a range of sectors.

The narrative doesn't downplay the difficulties that come with such quick technical advancement, though. We examine the issues of pricing and accessibility because some of NVIDIA's innovative technologies may put obstacles in the way of those who stand to gain the most. The book also explores how powerful GPUs affect the environment, emphasizing the continuous attempts to minimize the company's carbon footprint and develop sustainable solutions.

The story takes a look ahead and explores the fascinating but uncharted region of the future. We investigate the possibilities of the metaverse, an immersive virtual environment of the future driven by artificial intelligence and high-end computation. This article examines how NVIDIA has shaped this emerging digital environment and the opportunities and problems it may bring. The book explores various future technologies that could transform many aspects of our lives, like tailored learning experiences and advanced robotics, and shows how NVIDIA's innovations could lead to these kinds of breakthroughs.

Beyond the innovations in technology, the book provides an insight into the man who spearheaded the revolution in technology. Although Huang doesn't provide many details about his personal life, we look at the ones that are known and find that he is devoted to lifelong study, charitable work, and societal influence. This comprehensive perspective of Huang presents a picture of a well-rounded person motivated by goals not only in technology but also in using technology to advance humankind.

This preface opens the door to an interesting adventure. The tale of Jensen Huang and NVIDIA serves as a monument to the ability of human creativity to change the world, the value of visionary leadership, and the responsibility that comes with using technology. As we go through the pages more closely, we discover insightful information that can encourage the next generation to embrace innovation, question conventional wisdom, and work toward improving the world. This book is, above all, a call to action for everyone who dares to dream large and use technology to create a better future. It also serves as a tribute to the lasting legacy of Jensen Huang and NVIDIA and a celebration of human potential.

CHAPTER 1: EARLY LIFE AND ACADEMIC PURSUITS

The story of Jensen Huang starts on February 17, 1963, in Tainan, Taiwan. His early years were surrounded by a culture that valued education and fostered a sense of curiosity because he was born into a middle-class household. He was raised with a logical mind and an interest in mechanisms by his chemical engineer father, Huang Xing-tai. His mother, elementary school teacher Lo Tsai-hsiu, instilled in him a passion for education and a faith in the transformative power of information. The foundation of Huang's success in the future would be laid by these early influences.

Huang's early years in Taiwan were filled with a rich tapestry of modernism mixed with tradition. The vibrant port city of Tainan, which has a long history, provided a window into the island nation's distinctive fusion of Eastern and Western elements. The sights, sounds, and scents of a busy marketplace, with the aroma of street food vendors blending with the noise of haggling and pleasantries, are what Huang remembers from his early years. But within the walls of their small house, learning was highly valued. The evenings were spent reading books and having thought-provoking discussions while gathered around the dinner table. His fascination with electronics was fostered by his parents, who saw their son's innate curiosity and gave him basic tools and abandoned devices to play with. Disassembling vintage radios and clocks turned became a beloved past activity, a basic kind of inquiry that sparked an interest in learning about how technology functions from the inside out.

Huang's life unexpectedly changed at the age of five when his family moved to Thailand so that his father could pursue greater job prospects. He was introduced to a new language and culture as a result of this relocation, which he met with his usual curiosity. Thailand offered a sharp contrast to his life in Taiwan with its unique Buddhist customs and lively street life. Huang showed a remarkable capacity to navigate unfamiliar social and cultural contexts despite the initial language barrier. His early cultural immersion experience would come in very handy later in life, helping him to develop an appreciation for diversity and a global perspective.

However, there were challenges in living in Thailand. According to reports, the family experienced discrimination because of their race, but they overcame it by being resourceful and resilient. Huang's experiences during this period would subsequently influence his views on the value of cross-cultural dialogue and his empathy for immigrants.

When Huang was nine years old in 1972, his parents made a tough choice that would change Huang's life significantly. They sent him and his brother to live with an uncle in Tacoma, Washington, in the United States, to give their kids more educational possibilities. This choice was a crucial turning point in Huang's journey, driven by their unyielding devotion to their children's future.

Regretfully, the initial adjustment to life in the United States proved to be more difficult than expected. Huang's uncle had mistakenly put them at a religious reform school for "difficult" kids called Oneida Baptist Institute in rural Kentucky. This was hardly the elite boarding school they had imagined; instead, it was a sobering awakening. Huang has talked about the bullying he and his brother experienced as well as the regular tasks of cleaning toilets. Despite these setbacks, he developed a strong sense of resilience and a profound respect for his parents' sacrifices on his behalf throughout these formative years. He believes that these difficulties helped him develop a strong work ethic and a strong will to succeed—qualities that will be beneficial to him in the future.

After a year, their parents in Oregon found steady employment and they were at last reunited with them. After moving to Beaverton, a Portland suburb, Huang discovered a friendlier community.

After overcoming the difficulties and victories of his early life, Jensen Huang resumed his journey in the US with an emphasis on education. His time in Oregon's high school shaped his academic interests and laid the groundwork for his future contributions to the world of technology, igniting his growing interest in the subject.

Huang's new academic home was Aloha High School in Beaverton, a suburb of Portland. He initially struggled with language, but he soon adjusted to the American educational system, showing a natural talent for science and arithmetic. His teachers recognized his extraordinary potential and encouraged his intellectual curiosity, which allowed him to flourish in a stimulating school environment. Huang's love of technology was greatly sparked by instructors like Mr. Peterson, his computer science teacher. Mr. Peterson was able to go past Huang's reserved exterior and see his curiosity and desire to learn. He exposed him to the world of programming languages, gave him access to advanced computer science courses, and pushed him to learn more about computer architecture.

Huang's academic career, though, extended beyond the classroom. In the late 1970s, the field of personal computers was growing rapidly and attracted a great deal of interest. When the Apple II was released in 1977, it captivated his interest, and he read up on everything he could about this ground-breaking device. In an attempt to comprehend its internal workings, he devoted numerous hours to examining publications and manuals. In addition to expanding his technical expertise, this self-directed study gave him a lifelong habit of keeping up with the most recent developments in technology.

He was not limited to the computer world in his quest for knowledge. He took an active part in the school debate club, which helped him hone his communication abilities and cultivate a critical thinking style that would be very useful in his future profession. In addition, he developed a passion for philosophy and history, two subjects that extended his horizons and gave him a purpose outside of technology. He had the view that advances in technology need to be used for the benefit of society as a whole, and this would shape his vision for NVIDIA going forward.

During his high school years, a summer internship at a nearby semiconductor business was one of his most memorable experiences. Huang's initial introduction to the real world of semiconductor design and fabrication came during this internship. The complex dance of physics and engineering that went into making these little technological wonders enthralled him. Observing the complete procedure, ranging from the preliminary design phases to the intricate fabrication process, cemented his ambition to pursue a profession in electrical engineering. He saw this area as the ideal means of combining his interest in computers with his ambition to apply engineering concepts to the practical creation of solutions.

Huang enrolled in Oregon State University's esteemed electrical engineering school in 1979 at the extraordinary age of sixteen. Even though he excelled academically in high school, adjusting to college life brought with it new difficulties. He was surrounded by intelligent students from all over the nation, many of whom were from wealthier families. Huang was nevertheless driven ahead by his persistent resolve and strong work ethic. He threw himself into his studies, absorbing difficult ideas out of an unquenchable curiosity. Scholars such as computer scientist Dr. Richard Newton acknowledged Huang's aptitude and promise. Huang was given advanced courses by Dr. Newton, who also encouraged him to take part in research projects. These experiences helped Huang develop intellectually and improve his research techniques.

Throughout his undergraduate years, Huang explored his entrepreneurial mentality, but his studies remained his major priority. He co-founded a small business that specialized in computer hardware and software troubleshooting and provided consulting services to nearby businesses. Despite its small scale, this endeavor gave him important insights into the business management field and the difficulties involved in launching a new product or service. He gained knowledge about the value of customer service, marketing, and teamwork—skills that would be extremely useful in his future undertakings.

Outside of the classroom and his entrepreneurial endeavors, Huang was an active member of Oregon State's thriving engineering community. He became involved in computer science and electronics-focused student clubs, where he met others who shared his enthusiasm for technology and formed a network of like-minded friends. His sense of camaraderie and teamwork was cultivated by these interactions, which equipped him for the collaborative nature of employment in the tech sector. To stay up to date on the most recent developments and network with other ambitious engineers and business owners, he frequently went to industry conferences and seminars.

However, Huang did not have an easy time throughout his stay at Oregon State. He felt a great sense of duty to contribute to the household income as the oldest son of a family that had immigrated twice. He worked a part-time job and balanced his studies, frequently staying up late and early in the morning to make ends meet. These experiences taught him the value of endurance and hard effort, despite the financial burden. He gained efficient time management and prioritization skills.

His future leadership style would be influenced by his capacity to handle his hectic schedule. He picked up skills in task delegation, team member motivation, and stress tolerance. His academic and personal experiences at Oregon State helped to mold him into a well-rounded person who possesses the necessary abilities to successfully navigate the challenges of the working world in addition to technical knowledge.

Huang earned a Bachelor of Science in Electrical Engineering in 1984 from Oregon State University. He had learned a great deal and grown tremendously throughout his time at Oregon State. Along with improving his technical proficiency and comprehension of electrical engineering, he also acquired important leadership and communication abilities. Most significantly, he had come out with a clear plan for his future: to push the envelope of technology and develop ground-breaking ideas that would revolutionize how we communicate with computers.

Driven by aspiration and a desire to learn more, Huang decided to continue his education. His target was Stanford University, a prominent college known for its innovative research and supportive atmosphere for budding engineers and business owners. His drive to fully immerse himself in the realm of creativity was further spurred by Stanford's closeness to Silicon Valley, the epicenter of the tech industry. Admissions officers were drawn to his application because it was full of the passion and determination that had become his trademark. They saw in him not only a young man with exceptional academic ability but also one who was driven to change the world.

When Huang walked through Stanford University's doors in 1984, he started a new chapter in his academic career. Stanford provided an environment that was stimulating beyond anything he had ever encountered. He was surrounded by some of the most intelligent people working in electrical engineering and computer science. Professors such as the well-known computer architect Professor John Hennessy had a significant impact on his academic growth. Huang's critical thinking was pushed, his problem-solving abilities were developed, and he was exposed to the discipline of computer graphics—which would play a major role in Huang's future endeavors—by Professor Hennessy.

Huang was also able to work with top academics in the field and gain access to state-of-the-art research facilities thanks to Stanford. His developing enthusiasm for the possibility of hardware acceleration led him to enthusiastically participate in research initiatives on computer architecture and parallel processing. His technical understanding was enhanced by these research experiences, but they also gave him a strong scientific approach to problem-solving, which would be invaluable in his future commercial pursuits.

For Huang, Stanford meant more than just academics. Engaging in a dynamic student community, he fully submerged himself in a realm of thought leadership and inventive cooperation. He became involved in student organizations devoted to computer science and engineering, where he was able to connect with others who shared his enthusiasm for technology. His preparation for the collaborative nature of work in the IT industry was furthered by these interactions, which promoted a sense of camaraderie and teamwork. To stay up to date on the most recent developments in parallel processing and computer graphics, he frequently went to industry conferences and workshops. In addition to being exposed to state-of-the-art research, these conferences gave him the chance to network with influential members of the industry and possible partners.

CHAPTER 2: THE STANFORD CHAPTER

A crucial period in Jensen Huang's life was spent at Stanford University, where he developed both academically and the entrepreneurial mentality that would eventually inspire him to co-found NVIDIA. When he walked through the doors in 1984, he was surrounded by some of the most brilliant brains in electrical engineering and computer science. These outstanding people sparked his intellectual interest and led him to pursue ground-breaking computer graphics research, especially with access to state-of-the-art research facilities.

During Huang's tenure at Stanford, legendary computer architect Professor John Hennessy was one of the most important players. Huang was forced to think critically and creatively by Professor Hennessy, who also encouraged him to approach issues from novel perspectives. He gave him the valuable skill of a rigorous scientific approach to problem-solving, which would later become a defining characteristic of Huang's leadership style. Huang found great resonance in Professor Hennessy's computer architecture courses, especially about his emphasis on parallel processing. His later work on graphics processing units (GPUs), a technology that would completely transform the area of computer graphics, would be built around these ideas.

Professor David Wall, a computer scientist renowned for his groundbreaking work in computer graphics, was another significant person. Professor Wall gave Huang very helpful advice and mentoring. He encouraged Huang to further his research interests in computer graphics hardware acceleration after realizing his talent and potential. Huang's investigation into how specialized hardware may improve the speed of computer graphics programs was sparked by Professor Wall's research on graphics pipelines and rendering tricks.

Beyond these well-known individuals, Huang found a lively intellectual community at Stanford. Engaged in active participation in computer graphics and parallel processing research groups, he worked with bright graduate students who embraced innovation as he did. Through these exchanges, a culture of healthy competition and intellectual interchange was promoted, encouraging each other to create new concepts and improve upon old ones. To keep up with the most recent developments in graphics hardware and software, he frequently went to industry conferences and workshops. Through his encounters with prominent scholars and industry people, he gained insight into the opportunities and challenges that exist in the quickly developing field of computer graphics.

Creating a high-performance graphics pipeline for a flight simulator project was one of Huang's major Stanford assignments. He was able to put his theoretical understanding of parallel processing and computer graphics to use in this endeavor. He created a unique piece of hardware that greatly sped up the production of intricate 3D images, giving users of flight simulators a more realistic and engaging experience. The accomplishment of this project gave him invaluable insights into the real-world difficulties involved in creating and incorporating specialized hardware into current systems, in addition to confirming his belief in the possibilities of hardware acceleration.

The construction of a scalable architecture for parallel rendering was the subject of another research effort. To display complicated sceneries more quickly, this research looked into the potential benefits of using many CPUs cooperatively. The foundation for the creation of multi-core GPUs, a technology that would be essential to NVIDIA's future success, was created by this research.

Huang's postgraduate work at Stanford involved more than just research projects. In addition, he completed advanced courses in parallel processing, computer graphics, and computer architecture. His comprehension of the fundamental ideas behind the developments in computer graphics has grown as a result of these classes. He studied in-depth subjects including texture mapping, shading techniques, and 3D rendering algorithms, acquiring a thorough mastery of the whole graphics pipeline. This comprehensive understanding would come in very handy as he built and developed cutting-edge GPU architectures in the future.

Despite being fully engaged in Stanford's intellectually engaging atmosphere, Huang never lost sight of his business spirit. He saw that hardware acceleration could transform a variety of applications, including animation and video editing, scientific visualization, and medical imaging, in addition to flying simulators. He started to see a business focused on creating specialized graphics processors that would enable computer graphics to reach their full potential.

Huang's path to Stanford was not without difficulties, though. His resolve was put to the test by the grueling effort of graduate school and the financial strain of living in posh Silicon Valley. He used his technical skills to produce revenue while juggling part-time consultancy employment with his schooling. In addition to improving his financial circumstances, this experience gave him invaluable practical experience that enabled him to apply his academic knowledge to real-world issues that computer companies faced.

Huang earned a master's degree in electrical engineering in 1992 from Stanford University. His experience at Stanford had been life-changing. Along with honing his research techniques, critical thinking abilities, and network inside the tech business, he expanded his technical knowledge in computer graphics and computer architecture. Above all, his time at Stanford confirmed for him the promise of hardware acceleration and the revolutionary effects it could have on computers in the future.

With a strong base of knowledge and experience, a strong sense of entrepreneurial spirit, and a clear goal, Huang was prepared to start the next phase of his journey: the creation of NVIDIA. However, there were several obstacles in the way from academic research to business success. Huang would have to manage the difficulties of acquiring money, put together a strong team, and persuade a dubious market that his technology has revolutionary potential.

Huang's dissatisfaction with the shortcomings of the graphics hardware on the market gave rise to the original concept for NVIDIA. Central processing units (CPUs) were used in personal computers of the time to handle all processing activities, including graphics. This method hampered the visual fidelity and performance, which limited the possibilities of computer graphics applications. Huang thought he could usher in a new era of visual computing by creating specialized hardware used only for graphics processing.

His transformation from an inquisitive student who was fascinated by technology to a visionary leader in charge of a major international tech company is proof of the strength of tenacity, creativity, and an unwavering pursuit of a goal. The Stanford chapter helped him develop the entrepreneurial attitude that would enable him to transform the field of computer graphics and open the door for the advancement of high-performance computing, in addition to providing him with the necessary technical expertise and research abilities.

CHAPTER 3: EARLY CAREER AND INDUSTRY INSIGHTS

Although Jensen Huang's time at Stanford gave him the technical groundwork for his subsequent pursuits, his pre-Stanford work experiences were essential in molding his perspective on business and technology. These early ventures into engineering taught him important skills that would eventually play a key role in driving NVIDIA's success.

Soon after earning his bachelor's degree from Oregon State University in 1984, Huang began his first professional job. He was hired by well-known semiconductor company Advanced Micro Devices (AMD). He worked for AMD and was put in charge of the design team for microprocessors, which are intricate devices that act as computers' brains. Despite the short duration of his employment at AMD, he gained priceless knowledge about the real-world applications of chip design and manufacturing. He observed the painstaking process of turning silicon wafers into complex circuits, which required accuracy, teamwork, and a thorough comprehension of engineering and physics concepts.

Huang's next career destination was LSI Logic, a software engineering and semiconductor design company. In this position, he assumed a more varied role and worked on a range of projects involving software development, system integration, and hardware design. He was able to recognize the significance of a comprehensive approach to product development and the interconnectedness of technologies as a result of this increased exposure. He saw directly how firmware, software, and hardware needed to cooperate flawlessly to provide a useful and intuitive experience.

Even though they were brief, Huang's early professional experiences had a significant influence on his viewpoint. He gained an understanding of the value of cooperation, teamwork, and communication. He saw that the successful launch of intricate items required close collaboration among engineers, designers, and software developers. He also developed a profound respect for the manufacturing process, the complex balancing act between engineering and physics that turned raw materials into potent computing apparatuses.

But Huang also carried a sense of anger from his time at well-known companies. He was aware of the constraints imposed by working in big businesses, where innovation frequently happened slowly. He longed for a more dynamic setting in which he could more quickly bring his ideas from paper to reality. These encounters stoked his entrepreneurial zeal and planted the idea that he should find a business that values innovation and pushes limits.

In addition to the practical knowledge and technical expertise, Huang's early professional experiences were extremely influential in shaping his future computing vision. He became aware of the shortcomings of current technology while working on microprocessors, especially in graphics processing capacity. He saw that certain activities could be expedited by specialized technology, an idea that would eventually form the basis of NVIDIA's success with GPUs. Moreover, his involvement in a range of software development initiatives highlighted the significance of a user-centric methodology. He realized that without simple and user-friendly software to maximize its capabilities, even the most powerful hardware was useless.

Huang kept up with developments in the tech sector while attending Stanford and working on his master's degree. He saw how the market for personal computers was growing and how there was a growing need for programs that were more visually stimulating and immersive. He was aware of the shortcomings of the current graphics solutions and thought that the way people interacted with computers might be completely changed by his idea of dedicated graphics processors.

Huang's vision for computing's future was evident by the time he graduated from Stanford in 1992. In his idealized world, personal computers would serve as immersive platforms that could provide intricate simulations, rich multimedia experiences, and cutting-edge scientific visualizations, rather than merely being instruments for everyday tasks. He thought that this promise might be realized and a new era of visual computing brought about by specialized hardware, such as GPUs. Equipped with an abundance of technical expertise, real-world experience, and a fierce drive for entrepreneurship, Huang was prepared to realize his dream.

However, there were many obstacles in the way of realizing the vision and achieving financial success. Convincing potential investors of the feasibility of his ground-breaking plan was Huang's first obstacle. At the time, a lot of venture capitalists were dubious about the marketability of the relatively new idea of dedicated graphics processors. They questioned if the market for such a niche product was sufficiently established and whether it could hold its own against the integrated graphics solutions that were already on the market.

But Huang never wavered in his faith in his vision. He relentlessly pushed his concept, highlighting how GPUs may revolutionize computing and usher in a new era of visual processing. He maintained that graphics processing units (GPUs) will not only improve gaming but open up whole new applications in engineering, science, and design. He provided thorough technical details and industry analysis, creating an engaging vision of graphics technology's future.

Huang persevered for months, and it eventually paid off. A group of forward-thinking venture investors, including Sequoia Capital and Kleiner Perkins Caufield & Byers, provided him with $40 million in funding in 1993. With the startup money in hand, Huang brought together a group of bright engineers and computer scientists who were all driven by the same desire to innovate. Many of these early hires were people Huang had previously worked with on research projects at Stanford, people who shared his vision and were excited to be a part of something new.

The recently established NVIDIA, which took its name from the Hindu term meaning "intelligent vision," promoted a creative and cooperative atmosphere. Huang pushed the envelope of what was feasible, questioned preconceptions, and thought creatively as a team. He promoted an environment of open communication and teamwork, believing that engineers from various specialties could collaborate effectively.

Even though they were brief, Huang's early professional experiences were very important in determining how he approached technology and business. He gained knowledge about the value of cooperation, teamwork, and a user-centric mindset. He saw firsthand the drawbacks of current technology as well as the difficulties in commercializing novel concepts. These encounters stoked his spirit of entrepreneurship and prepared him for his current role as CEO of NVIDIA, a firm that keeps pushing the limits of graphics technology and influencing computing trends.

CHAPTER 4: THE BIRTH OF INNOVATION

It was 1993, a historic year that saw the founding of NVIDIA, a company that would completely transform the computer graphics industry. Driven by his steadfast faith in the capabilities of hardware acceleration and his background in the technology sector, Jensen Huang set out on a daring entrepreneurial expedition. This chapter dives into the history of NVIDIA, examining the idea exchange that resulted in the company's formation, the early obstacles the startup experienced, and the early triumphs that solidified its position as the industry leader in GPU sales.

The narrative of NVIDIA's founding starts in a less opulent location—Denny's roadside cafe in East San Jose—rather than in the boardrooms of Silicon Valley behemoths. Here, Huang met the two gifted engineers who would join him in this audacious endeavor, Curtis Priem and Chris Malachowsky. Priem and

Malachowsky were enthralled with Huang's contagious energy and distinct vision for the advancement of graphics technology. With his extensive background at IBM and Sun Microsystems, Priem was a seasoned graphics chip designer who contributed a plethora of technical know-how. An engineer with experience at Sun Microsystems, Malachowsky had a strong grasp of system design and integration—two areas that were essential to realizing Huang's vision.

The three founded NVIDIA because they were driven by a common love of invention and a conviction in the revolutionary power of GPUs. Their ambition was to establish a business that would focus on creating specialized graphics processing units that would enable computer graphics to reach their full potential. In the beginning, they concentrated on the growing PC market since it was becoming more and more obvious how limited the current graphics solutions were. Professional users wanted greater visual fidelity in design and engineering applications, gamers wanted better gaming, and multimedia aficionados wanted richer experiences. GPUs, according to Huang, Priem, and Malachowsky, might meet these demands and bring in a new era of visual computing.

Nevertheless, obtaining finance turned out to be a major challenge. Huang persevered for months, and it eventually paid off. A group of forward-thinking venture investors, including Sequoia Capital and Kleiner Perkins Caufield & Byers, provided the three with $40 million in funding in 1993. Upon receiving the seed funding, NVIDIA formally became an incorporated company. The term "Nvidya," which is drawn from Hinduism, means "intelligent vision."

The recently established NVIDIA promoted a creative and cooperative atmosphere. Ever the motivating boss, Huang pushed his group to think creatively, question preconceptions, and beyond the bounds of what was thought to be feasible. He promoted an environment of open communication and teamwork, believing that engineers from various specialties could collaborate effectively. Many of the initial hires were Stanford researchers and classmates of Huang's, people who shared his vision and were excited to be involved in an innovative project.

The NV1, a cutting-edge graphics processing unit (GPU) created especially for the PC market, was NVIDIA's initial product. When compared to previous graphics solutions, the NV1 provided noticeably faster performance and better image quality. This resulted in enhanced visual fidelity for professional graphics software, more immersive multimedia applications, and fluid gameplay for gamers.

The NV1 launch, nevertheless, wasn't without its problems. The lack of early drivers and software support impeded the technology's initial uptake. To fully utilize the NV1's capabilities, games and apps had to be specially customized, which required time and cooperation from software developers. To resolve these problems, Huang and his colleagues collaborated with game developers to make sure their games operated properly on the NV1 architecture and released updated drivers.

Notwithstanding these initial difficulties, gamers and graphics fans ultimately came to appreciate the NV1's higher performance. Demand for the product was driven by favorable evaluations and recommendations from friends and family. A new era of visual computing was ushered in by NVIDIA's rapid ascension to the top of the emerging GPU market.

Huang's vision was confirmed by the NV1's early success, which also cemented NVIDIA's leadership in computer graphics. The business had not only recognized a significant market need, but it had also put together a brilliant team that could produce a ground-breaking product. This chapter has examined the history of NVIDIA, emphasizing the idea exchange that resulted in the firm's formation, the difficulties the company first encountered, and the early achievements that helped the company go forward and become a leader in the industry.

But Huang and his NVIDIA colleagues knew that a single product wouldn't be enough to maintain success. They were dedicated to never-ending innovation and were always pushing the limits of GPU technology. NVIDIA produced several progressively potent and adaptable GPUs after the NV1, appealing to a broader spectrum of consumers.

When the GeForce series of GPUs was introduced in 1999, it was primarily aimed at the growing gaming business. These graphics processors provide gamers with fluid gaming, breathtaking images, and immersive experiences by offering unparalleled performance and cutting-edge capabilities. High-end graphics were swiftly associated with the GeForce series, making NVIDIA the preferred brand for PC gamers.

NVIDIA realized that GPUs could be used for more than just gaming in business applications. In 1998, the Quadro series of GPUs was released to meet the demands of scientists, engineers, and designers. With the help of these professional-grade GPUs, users could construct intricate 3D models, run sophisticated simulations, and view enormous datasets thanks to their improved performance, larger memory capacity, and unique capabilities. Workflows in industries including media and entertainment, engineering, architecture, and scientific research were transformed by the Quadro series.

In addition to adding new products to its lineup, NVIDIA concentrated on creating software tools and

APIs (Application Programming Interfaces) that would allow its GPUs to reach their maximum potential. When NVIDIA CUDA architecture was introduced in 2006, it revolutionized the field. Thanks to CUDA, programmers may now use GPUs' parallel processing capacity for activities other than graphics by utilizing general-purpose computing on GPUs (GPGPU). This strengthened NVIDIA's position as a leader in high-performance computing by creating new opportunities for financial modeling, scientific computing, artificial intelligence, and machine learning.

Not only were NVIDIA's early accomplishments a result of ground-breaking technology, but they also demonstrated Huang's style of leadership. He pushed staff to take chances and think creatively by fostering an innovative and collaborative culture. He promoted a user-centric strategy and solicited feedback from scientists, designers, and gamers regularly to make sure NVIDIA's products met their changing needs. To give customers a smooth and optimized experience, he also recognized the value of establishing a robust ecosystem around NVIDIA's GPUs through partnerships with game creators, hardware producers, and software developers.

NVIDIA has become a dominant player in the GPU market by the early 2000s. The corporation had completely changed the way people interacted with computers with its cutting-edge devices and dedication to software development and ecosystem building. Through cutting-edge scientific discoveries and immersive gaming experiences, NVIDIA's GPUs were revolutionizing a variety of sectors and pushing the envelope of what was conceivable. But the company's adventure was far from ended.

CHAPTER 5: THE RISE OF THE GPU

The history of computers underwent a sea change when NVIDIA invented the graphics processing unit (GPU). This chapter explores the history of the first GPU, its effects on the graphics and gaming industries, and the major product introductions and turning points that established NVIDIA as a pioneer in GPU technology.

Central processing units (CPUs) were responsible for all computer processing, including graphics, before the invention of GPUs. This method hindered the potential of gaming, design, and other graphics-intensive sectors by limiting the visual fidelity and performance of graphics applications. Seeing this restriction, Jensen Huang and the NVIDIA team imagined a processor that was just used for graphics processing. The world's first commercially accessible GPU, the NV1, was the result of this ambition and was released in 1998.

The NV1 signified a noteworthy advancement in graphics technology. In comparison to earlier integrated graphics technologies, it provided better performance, showcasing increased frame rates, quicker rendering times, and better image quality. This resulted in enhanced visual fidelity for professional graphics software, more immersive multimedia applications, and fluid gameplay for gamers. Unquestionably, the NV1 had a significant impact and helped to usher in a new era of visual computing.

One of the first sectors to see the revolutionary potential of GPUs was the gaming industry. The gaming experience was completely changed by the improved graphical capabilities provided by the NV1 and later NVIDIA GeForce GPUs. Richer sceneries, finer textures, and intricate lighting effects could now be found in games, giving gamers a more realistic and immersive experience. Another catalyst for this change was NVIDIA's dedication to working with game creators. Through the provision of development tools and the optimization of their GPUs for particular game engines, NVIDIA made sure that games could fully utilize GPU technology. By working closely together, creators of both hardware and software created a vibrant gaming community and expanded the frontiers of interactive entertainment.

GPUs had an impact on other graphics-intensive industries in addition to gaming. When the NVIDIA Quadro series was introduced in 1998, it was intended to meet the demands of scientists, engineers, and designers. For operations like 3D modeling, animation, and video editing, these professional-grade GPUs provided noticeably better performance than CPUs. Scientists could view enormous datasets in never-before-seen detail, engineers could carry out intricate simulations with more accuracy, and architects could produce more realistic and accurate building models. Professionals can work more productively, iterate more quickly, and push the limits of creativity and innovation in their fields thanks to GPUs.

The NV1 and Quadro series' popularity only served to further NVIDIA's unrelenting quest for innovation. Over the years, the business developed several ground-breaking GPUs, with each generation outperforming the previous one in terms of functionality, features, and performance. Notable events included the release of the NVIDIA Tesla series in 2008, which was created especially for high-performance computing applications like artificial intelligence and machine learning, and the launch of the GeForce GTX 880 in 2014, which brought in the era of virtual reality (VR) gaming.

More realistic graphics and quicker rendering were not the only factors contributing to the GPU's rise. It radically altered the way information was processed by computers. With the release of their CUDA architecture in 2006, NVIDIA opened up the possibility of general-purpose computing on GPUs (GPGPU). Programmers are now able to use GPUs' parallel processing capacity for a variety of activities beyond graphics, including scientific computing, financial modeling, and artificial intelligence research, thanks to this paradigm change. GPUs have evolved from being primarily used to speed up graphics to being potent instruments for the research and development of new technologies.

However, there were certain difficulties with GPUs' ascent. The complexity of programming for these potent processors was one of the main obstacles. The parallel processing design of GPUs was not well suited to traditional CPU programming models. In response, NVIDIA created libraries and tools like CUDA, which gave programmers an easier method to take advantage of GPU capabilities. In addition to democratizing access to GPU computing, these initiatives created a thriving developer community that keeps pushing the limits of this technology.

The growing heat generation and power consumption of GPUs posed another obstacle to their broad adoption. GPUs need more power to run as their power increases. This posed a problem for software developers who had to optimize code to reduce power consumption as well as hardware designers who had to create effective cooling solutions. By utilizing cutting-edge design strategies and power management tools, NVIDIA overcame this difficulty and made sure that their GPUs maintained energy efficiency while delivering peak performance.

Notwithstanding these difficulties, GPUs have a lot more potential advantages than disadvantages. Exciting new applications have been made possible by the GPUs' ever-increasing processing power and adaptability. GPUs emerged as the workhorses of deep learning algorithms in the field of artificial intelligence (AI), allowing scientists to create increasingly sophisticated and potent AI models. GPUs revolutionized scientific computing by speeding up simulations and data analysis, enabling researchers to address unsolvable issues. GPUs have also been adopted by the financial sector, which has improved the accuracy and efficiency of financial processes by using them for activities like fraud detection and risk modeling.

GPUs seem to have an even brighter future. NVIDIA is still making significant R&D investments, pushing the limits of GPU architecture, and discovering new computing frontiers. Artificial intelligence is one promising field. GPU power will become ever more critical as AI models grow more complicated. To speed up AI tasks, NVIDIA is creating specialized hardware, such as the Tensor Core architecture. Additionally, GPU power and versatility will continue to be critical to breakthroughs in fields like cloud gaming and high-performance computing.

The development of the GPU has revolutionized the computing industry. GPUs have completely transformed how humans interact with computers and approach challenging tasks. They have revolutionized the gaming and graphics industries and powered cutting-edge developments in AI and scientific computing. NVIDIA has been a key player in this change with its innovative spirit and persistent dedication to research and development. GPUs are expected to become increasingly more influential in the future, helping to shape the rapidly changing field of technology.

CHAPTER 6: LEADERSHIP AND INNOVATION

The transformation of Jensen Huang from an inquisitive student who was fascinated by technology to the visionary head of a multinational tech company is proof of the strength of tenacity, creativity, and the unwavering pursuit of a goal. This chapter explores Huang's concept of business and leadership, focusing on how he has led NVIDIA to achieve major technological achievements and developed an innovative culture within the company. Huang's leadership is rooted in his profound knowledge of technology and his sincere enthusiasm for its potential to enhance lives. With his combination of academic training and early industry experience, he has developed a special kind of technical expertise and sharp business sense that has helped NVIDIA become a leader in the IT sector. But Huang's leadership goes well beyond his aptitude for technology. He is well known for his captivating demeanor, contagious energy, and capacity to uplift and encourage his group.

His constant faith in the potential of innovation is one of his guiding principles as a leader. He encourages staff at NVIDIA to think creatively and collaboratively, to question conventional wisdom, and to push the envelope of what is considered achievable. He encourages experimentation and deliberate risk-taking among his team members, creating an atmosphere in which failure is viewed as a teaching opportunity rather than a setback. The creation of ground-breaking technology like the GPU and its ensuing applications in numerous fields have been made possible by this innovative culture, which has played a significant role in NVIDIA's success. Huang's dedication to assembling a capable team is another quality that distinguishes his leadership. He understands that teamwork and the combined knowledge of a varied staff are essential for creativity to flourish. He aggressively seeks out gifted scientists, engineers, and programmers from all around the world, encouraging an environment of candor and respect for one another. Huang thinks it's critical to support his staff members' professional development by giving them chances to advance as leaders in their own right.

Another quality that has distinguished Huang's leadership is his willingness to take measured chances. Long before the market adopted GPUs, he saw their promise, and he persistently supported this technology in the face of doubt from financiers and business insiders. In a similar vein, his bold choice to allocate significant funds to artificial intelligence R&D at the beginning of the 2000s established NVIDIA as a frontrunner in this quickly expanding industry. Huang's ability to take calculated risks, together with his good judgment and strategic vision, has been crucial in guiding NVIDIA's success going forward.

Analyzing the noteworthy technological advances made possible by Huang's direction paints a vivid picture of his influence on NVIDIA. The progress of the GPU, as described in earlier chapters, is evidence of his vision and technical prowess. Huang has been in charge of developing potent AI processors such as the Tensor Core architecture, which is intended to speed up deep learning algorithms, in addition to GPUs. Under Huang's direction, NVIDIA has also made great progress in the field of self-driving cars with its DRIVE platform, which provides hardware and software solutions for these vehicles.

Others disagree with Huang's leadership. Some contend that his emphasis on innovative technologies may obscure more customer-focused issues. For instance, casual gamers or enthusiasts may find it difficult to purchase certain NVIDIA GPUs due to their high price. Additionally, developers outside of specialist domains may have difficulties due to the intricacy of programming for GPUs. Huang and NVIDIA are always trying to solve these problems and improve the usability and accessibility of their technologies.

The technology developed by NVIDIA has far-reaching effects outside of the computer graphics and gaming industries. These days, GPUs are essential to scientific study because they let scientists work on challenging issues in areas like astronomy, climate modeling, and medicine. GPUs are speeding up drug discovery and medical imaging analysis in the healthcare industry, which is resulting in the creation of tailored medicine and better patient care. NVIDIA's DRIVE platform is assisting in laying the foundation for autonomous vehicle technology, which has the potential to transform transportation and boost road safety.

As time goes on, NVIDIA's technology appears to have countless possible uses. Thanks to the capability of powerful GPUs, artificial intelligence research has the potential to change a wide range of industries and profoundly impact our future. The potential impact is enormous, ranging from customizing learning experiences to transforming manufacturing processes.

Beyond just the technical components, Huang's leadership has had a significant influence on the tech sector as a whole. Because of NVIDIA's success with GPUs, innovation in the entire semiconductor industry has increased, encouraging other businesses to create graphics processors that are more potent and adaptable. Moreover, the evolution of artificial intelligence in multiple domains has been accelerated by NVIDIA's investment in research and development. In addition to revolutionizing NVIDIA, Huang's ideas and leadership have inspired and shaped the course of the IT sector as a whole.

Innovation and advancement at NVIDIA have been propelled forward under Jensen Huang's leadership. NVIDIA has risen to the top of the tech sector because of his vision, ability to assemble a solid team, and encouragement of creativity. The company's technological innovations, which range from AI processors and GPUs to self-driving car technologies, are significantly influencing many facets of our lives. Huang's leadership will surely be essential in determining how technology develops and affects society in the future as NVIDIA keeps pushing the envelope of what is feasible.

CHAPTER 7: EXPANDING HORIZONS

Although the creation of the GPU revolutionized computer graphics, Jensen Huang's ambition for the firm has always extended well beyond that. This chapter examines how NVIDIA strategically moved into the fields of deep learning and artificial intelligence (AI), how it used partnerships and strategic acquisitions to drive growth, and how it helped to advance the development of autonomous vehicles and other industries.

GPUs are becoming more and more versatile and powerful, making them suitable for use in areas other than graphics. In the early 2000s, NVIDIA started investigating the use of GPUs for AI and deep learning applications after realizing this potential. Massive data sets and intricate calculations are essential for deep learning algorithms, a type of artificial intelligence, to continuously learn and advance. GPUs' parallel processing architecture was a big help in speeding up these computationally demanding jobs.

The release of the CUDA architecture in 2006 was a turning point in this evolution. A framework for using GPU power for more than simply graphics was made available to programmers via CUDA. This ushered in a new phase of AI research since it allowed scientists to train sophisticated deep-learning models more quickly and effectively by utilizing GPU power.

The creation of specialist AI hardware, such as the Tensor Core Architecture in 2018, further cemented this strategic shift towards AI. With features like Tensor Cores, which dramatically speed up matrix multiplication operations—a crucial building component of many deep learning algorithms—these processors were created expressly to excel at deep learning workloads. In the quickly expanding field of artificial intelligence, NVIDIA established itself as a pioneer by providing not only potent GPUs but also specialized AI hardware.

NVIDIA strengthened its AI capabilities through collaborations and strategic acquisitions in addition to internal development. 2019 saw NVIDIA acquire Mellanox Technologies, a pioneer in high-performance networking technologies, giving it the foundation it needed to develop a powerful AI computing platform. Furthermore, NVIDIA's AI hardware and software tools were widely accessible and used by academics and developers thanks to relationships with top cloud providers like as Microsoft Azure and Amazon Web Services. This mix of strategic acquisitions, cooperative alliances, and organic growth propelled NVIDIA's ascent to prominence in the AI industry.

The technology developed by NVIDIA has far-reaching effects outside of the conventional computing world. The development of autonomous vehicles is one of the most intriguing applications. The DRIVE platform from NVIDIA offers the necessary hardware and software for autonomous vehicles. To analyze picture and sensor data in real-time and enable autonomous vehicles to sense their environment, make navigational decisions, and drive safely, the DRIVE platform makes use of strong GPUs and AI processors. With the potential to transform transportation and improve road safety as well as reduce traffic congestion, NVIDIA's innovations are helping to usher in a new era of transportation.

Technology from NVIDIA also has an impact on a wide range of other sectors. AI-powered medical imaging analysis, made possible by NVIDIA GPUs, is revolutionizing the healthcare industry by enabling earlier diagnosis and more individualized treatment regimens for patients. NVIDIA's technology is advancing scientific innovation and discovery in the field of research by enabling scientists to take on challenging issues in areas like materials science, genetics, and climate modeling. NVIDIA's GPUs are being used by creative industries like media and entertainment for tasks including content development, animation, and video editing.

There are obstacles in NVIDIA's path as it expands into AI and other different applications. The potential ethical ramifications of AI are a significant worry. As AI systems grow more potent and self-governing, concerns about accountability, transparency, and bias surface. By defining AI ethical guidelines and encouraging appropriate development techniques, NVIDIA has started to address these concerns. The business understands how critical it is to make sure that its technology is applied ethically and advances humankind's future.

One additional problem is the dynamic nature of technology. To keep ahead of the curve, NVIDIA needs to develop and adapt all the time. The business makes significant R&D investments, pushing the limits of AI algorithms, software development, and chip design. Furthermore, NVIDIA promotes an environment of cooperation and transparent innovation by collaborating with scholars, researchers, and other business titans to create cutting-edge innovations. In the rapidly evolving tech world, NVIDIA makes sure its technology is impactful and relevant by embracing constant learning and adaptation.

The technology developed by NVIDIA appears to have infinite applications. NVIDIA's GPUs and specialized AI hardware will be essential in driving the next generation of intelligent devices and self-governing systems as AI develops further. The potential impact is enormous, ranging from personalizing educational experiences to altering manufacturing processes.

With its move outside graphics processing units, NVIDIA has created a plethora of new opportunities. Through the adoption of AI, deep learning, and other advanced technologies, the organization persists in pushing the frontiers of innovation. NVIDIA's dedication to collaborative learning, responsible development, and ongoing learning sets it apart as a pioneer in influencing the direction of technology, even in the face of ongoing obstacles. Its technology can change entire industries, enhance people's lives, and pave the way for a better future for everybody. The world is excitedly awaiting the ground-breaking discoveries and revolutionary applications that NVIDIA's unwavering quest for innovation will surely produce as it begins its new chapter.

CHAPTER 8: CHALLENGES AND CONTROVERSIES

NVIDIA has seen its fair share of difficulties and controversy during its ascent to prominence in the tech sector. This chapter explores the challenges that NVIDIA has encountered, ranging from managing market forces and industry competitiveness to dealing with failures and scandals. It also looks at the business's persistent adaptability and resilience, which are important components of its success going forward.

NVIDIA faces several significant problems, one of which is navigating the strong competition that exists within the semiconductor business. Although NVIDIA has made a name for itself in the GPU industry, it still has to contend with fierce competition from well-established firms like AMD and up-and-coming startups hoping to make a name for themselves. This rivalry encourages innovation by driving manufacturers to continuously create GPUs that are more potent, economical, and efficient. But it also means that NVIDIA needs to play smart, making sure that it stays ahead of the competition with innovative technologies, smart alliances, and a user-centered approach.

In addition to direct rivalry, NVIDIA is under pressure from shifting market dynamics. Global economic trends, the frequency with which new gaming consoles are released, the popularity of mining cryptocurrencies, and other factors can all have a significant impact on the demand for GPUs. NVIDIA has proven that it is capable of reacting to these variations by modifying its product lineup and marketing plans to meet changing consumer demands. For example, the business has effectively broadened its clientele to include professionals in design, engineering, and scientific research in addition to gamers. The impact of market swings in any one industry is lessened thanks to this diversity.

NVIDIA also faces difficulties in handling disputes and defeats. The effect that mining cryptocurrencies have on the environment is one such dispute. GPUs are criticized for their part in the proof-of-work mining process because these algorithms are energy-intensive and are used in several cryptocurrencies. In response, NVIDIA has created GPUs that use less energy and is looking at forming alliances with cryptocurrency businesses to support environmentally friendly mining methods.

NVIDIA has been under fire for the exorbitant price of its top-tier GPUs. Even though these GPUs have unmatched performance, casual gamers or those on a tight budget may not be able to afford them. In response, NVIDIA provides a selection of GPUs at different price points to accommodate a wide range of customer demands and financial constraints. The business also makes significant investments in cloud gaming technologies, which can give users access to powerful GPUs without requiring costly hardware acquisitions.

Despite these difficulties and disputes, NVIDIA has proven to be remarkably adaptive and resilient in the face of hardship. The organization promotes a resilient culture and encourages staff members to grow from setbacks. This tenacity is demonstrated by NVIDIA's persistent R&D expenditures, dedication to cultivating a robust and diverse workforce, and openness to investigating novel markets and technological applications.

It's critical to recognize that there are several current, intricate debates concerning NVIDIA. For example, ethical questions about the development of AI continue to be a major obstacle. Concerns concerning potential biases in algorithms, the explainability of AI decision-making processes, and the potential misuse of AI for malevolent reasons emerge as NVIDIA's AI technology grows more robust and pervasive. By creating AI ethics guidelines, encouraging responsible development practices, and working with researchers and policymakers to create frameworks for safe and ethical AI development, NVIDIA is actively addressing these challenges.

Ensuring the ethical procurement of materials for NVIDIA products is another continuous issue. To guarantee fair labor conditions and reduce environmental effects, ethical sourcing techniques are essential in the electronics industry's intricate worldwide supply chain. To address this issue, NVIDIA has worked with suppliers to encourage moral behavior through the supply chain and has put in place regulations for responsible sourcing. Nonetheless, in the always-changing digital scene, ongoing attention to detail and flexibility are required to manage the challenges of global sourcing.

Going forward, NVIDIA is probably going to encounter more difficulties as the technology industry develops. New technologies such as quantum computing have the potential to challenge GPU dominance as it is. On the other hand, NVIDIA's track record of innovation and flexibility indicates that the business is well-positioned to meet these upcoming obstacles and keep leading the way in technological growth.

From negotiating business competition to addressing ethical concerns, NVIDIA has encountered several difficulties. However, NVIDIA has become a leader in influencing the direction of computing due to its unrelenting dedication to pushing the boundaries of technology, its ability to make smart decisions, and its capacity to learn from mistakes. The corporation will undoubtedly encounter new opportunities and problems as it pushes into uncharted territory like artificial intelligence, self-driving cars, and the promise of the metaverse. But given its track record and dedication to ethical growth, NVIDIA seems well-suited to handle these challenges and carry on influencing technology for the good of all.

CHAPTER 9: RECOGNITION AND LEGACY

During his tenure as NVIDIA's CEO, Jensen Huang has shown incredible inventiveness and leadership. This chapter explores the accolades and acclaim he received, his contributions to society and the larger tech world, his thoughts on his legacy, and his future goals for NVIDIA.

Huang's accomplishments are not underappreciated. Throughout his career, he has been bestowed with a plethora of accolades, such as Ernst & Young's 1999 Entrepreneur of the Year in High Technology Award, the Semiconductor Industry Association's highest accolade, the Robert N. Noyce Award, in 2021, and a consistent ranking among the world's top CEOs by Fortune and Harvard Business Review. These honors provide witness to his leadership, vision, and the revolutionary impact he had on NVIDIA.

In addition to receiving praise on his own, Huang's leadership has promoted an innovative culture outside of

NVIDIA. He collaborates with researchers, policymakers, and other industry executives to shape the future of technology as an active member of the tech community. He encourages young people to seek jobs in science, technology, engineering, and math by being a strong supporter of STEM education. Huang's dedication to developing the next round of innovators guarantees a steady stream of talent that will advance the IT sector.

Huang has goals that go beyond the IT sector. He understands how NVIDIA's technology can help with some of the most important problems facing the globe today. NVIDIA actively backs projects about healthcare, education, and climate change. For example, the company's GPUs are being used to tailor learning experiences, expedite medical research, and create more effective renewable energy solutions. Through the use of its technologies for social good, NVIDIA is making a positive impact on everyone's future.

Huang does, however, engage in active philanthropy. He and his spouse, Lori, are well-known for their philanthropic endeavors, especially in the fields of healthcare and education. They have backed programs that encourage STEM education and give impoverished communities access to technology. Huang's dedication to giving back is a reflection of his aim to use technology for good social effect in addition to business success.

It's also important to take into account his charitable endeavors. Concern over the possibility of job displacement is growing as automation and artificial intelligence continues to change the nature of labor. Huang's dedication to education may enable him to lead innovative programs that provide people with the tools they need to succeed in the changing labor market. Furthermore, his interest in healthcare may lead to sponsorship for investigations into personalized medicine or AI-powered diagnostics.

When considering his legacy, Huang is probably going to be seen as a visionary leader who completely changed the computing industry. His unshakeable faith in the potential of GPUs and his tireless quest for invention has revolutionized a wide range of industries, including scientific research, healthcare, and autonomous vehicles, in addition to gaming and graphics. For Huang, though, the narrative is far from finished. He keeps an eye on the future and pushes the envelope of what's feasible as the leader of NVIDIA.

It's critical to recognize that there may be disagreements on Huang's legacy. His emphasis on cutting-edge technology has the power to eclipse worries about cost and accessibility. Some people who would profit from NVIDIA goods' capabilities may find them prohibitively expensive. Furthermore, the environmental impact of powerful GPUs is questioned due to their high energy usage. To make sure that their technology benefits a larger audience and helps assure a sustainable future, Huang and NVIDIA will need to address these issues going ahead.

From a historical perspective, Huang's accomplishments are indisputable. He changed the computing industry, grew a small startup into a multinational tech juggernaut, and keeps pushing the envelope of what's possible. His steadfast faith in the ability of technology to enhance lives acts as a compass for NVIDIA as it works to mold a future in which technological innovations benefit all people.

There is a chance that NVIDIA's foray into the metaverse will have both advantageous and harmful effects. The metaverse has the potential to completely transform how we communicate, collaborate, and learn. But worries about addiction, privacy, and the possibility of socioeconomic inequality continue. Huang and NVIDIA will be instrumental in guiding the metaverse's evolution and making sure it turns into a constructive and inclusive digital future.

Huang has high expectations for NVIDIA. He sees the business having a major influence on the development of the metaverse, an immersive virtual environment of the future driven by artificial intelligence and high-performance computing. Additionally, he believes that artificial intelligence (AI) has a ton of potential and that NVIDIA's technology will propel advances in robotics, customized medicine, and intelligent technologies that will enhance our lives in a variety of ways.

Technology has never been the same since Jensen Huang took the helm at NVIDIA. His ability to inspire and forge a solid team, along with his vision, has driven NVIDIA to the forefront of innovation. The company's technological innovations, which range from AI processors to GPUs, are significantly influencing many facets of our lives. One thing is certain, though, as Huang continues to lead NVIDIA toward even more exciting times ahead: his legacy as a visionary leader and his dedication to using technology to create a better future will serve as an inspiration to future generations.

CONCLUSION

Beyond technology, Jensen Huang's journey through the heart of Silicon Valley is an engrossing tale. It is evidence of the transforming force of unyielding ambition, a never-ending quest for invention, and a firm conviction that technology can fundamentally alter our world. This last chapter considers the most important lessons learned from Huang's extraordinary journey, the long-lasting influence of his leadership on NVIDIA, and the promising prospects that await as the company forges ahead into unexplored future domains.

Huang's unrelenting confidence in the potential of technology to help lives is the driving force behind his success. His early interest in electronics and his groundbreaking work in GPUs and AI are just two examples of how frequently he has shown a creative approach and pushed the envelope of what is achievable. Because of his powerful combination of technical know-how, strategic vision, and contagious energy, he has created an innovative culture at NVIDIA that has drawn and inspired some of the best minds in the business. NVIDIA's innovations have far-reaching effects outside of the computer graphics and gaming industries. These days, GPUs are crucial to medical research, scientific advancement, and the creation of driverless cars. The possibilities for using NVIDIA's technology appear to be endless. AI and high-performance computers have the potential to change many facets of our environment, from manufacturing processes to personalized learning experiences.

However, there are complications with Huang's leadership. His emphasis on cutting-edge technology may cause some people to question accessibility and affordability. Some people who would profit from NVIDIA goods' capabilities may find them prohibitively expensive. Furthermore, there needs to be constant work towards sustainable solutions due to the energy consumption of strong GPUs. NVIDIA will need to pay close attention to ethical issues about privacy, addiction, and potential socioeconomic imbalances as it explores new horizons like the metaverse. To guarantee that

NVIDIA's technology serves a larger audience and contributes to a bright future for everybody, it will be imperative to address these issues.

Beyond his accomplishments at NVIDIA, Huang is a well-rounded person motivated by a desire to have a positive societal influence. This is demonstrated by his dedication to humanitarian activities and his lifelong learning philosophy. He demonstrates his passion for enabling future generations to influence a brighter tomorrow via his support of STEM education projects and his focus on encouraging access to technology in underserved communities.

Huang's values, work-life balance philosophy, and commitment to continuing learning will surely continue to inform his leadership style and strategic choices as NVIDIA navigates the rapidly changing digital industry. Huang's personal experience will influence his professional endeavors, whether it is because of his love of science which drives him to explore new technologies, or because his charitable endeavors change to meet new difficulties in the future.

Jensen Huang's tale serves as a monument to the capacity of the human spirit to pursue great dreams, push limits, and build better futures. This narrative urges the next generation to embrace innovation, question conventional wisdom, and work toward improving the world. It is a beacon of inspiration. The legacy of Jensen Huang and NVIDIA serves as a potent reminder that, as we stand on the cusp of a new era propelled by artificial intelligence (AI), the metaverse, and technological developments beyond our current comprehension, the future is something to be created rather than something to be foretold. Furthermore, technology has the power to create a better future for everybody if it is used with the correct vision, commitment, and responsible growth.

Still, this is not the conclusion of the story. Jensen Huang's impact will not go away as new chapters in the ever-changing story of technology are written. His impact on the industry, his inspiration for upcoming generations of inventors, and the ground-breaking innovations NVIDIA pioneered will all contribute to shaping the technological landscape for years to come. The path taken by Jensen Huang and NVIDIA is a story that will surely inspire and enchant people for years to come. It is a monument to the transformational power of human invention.

The history of Huang is still being written. He has made a name for himself in Silicon Valley as a visionary leader who has changed the face of computing and AI forever. His steadfast commitment, astute strategic thinking, and contagious enthusiasm have catapulted NVIDIA to the forefront of technological advancement. Looking ahead, the adventure that Jensen Huang and NVIDIA started has just begun. The opportunities that lie ahead are enormous and thrilling, and their achievements could have a lasting effect on how human history is written for future generations. This is a story that should inspire everyone who dares to dream large, push boundaries, and pursue a vision for a better future—not only aspiring innovators and leaders.

www.ingramcontent.com/pod-product-compliance
Lightning Source LLC
Chambersburg PA
CBHW050235230526
45470CB00005B/1962